Happy
NEW YEAR

ABBIE MERCER

PowerKiDS press.

New York

For Suzi Power

Published in 2008 by The Rosen Publishing Group, Inc.
29 East 21st Street, New York, NY 10010

First Edition

Editor: Amelie von Zumbusch
Book Design: Julio Gil
Photo Researcher: Nicole Pristash

Photo Credits: Cover, p. 1 © www.istockphoto.com/Andrew Rich; pp. 5, 7, 9, 17 © Getty Images; pp. 11, 15, 19, 21 © Shutterstock.com; p. 11 (inset) © www.istockphoto.com/Joseph Brewster; p. 13 © www.istockphoto.com/Bonnie Jacobs.

Library of Congress Cataloging-in-Publication Data

Mercer, Abbie.
  Happy New Year / Abbie Mercer. — 1st ed.
      p. cm. — (Holiday fun)
  Includes index.
  ISBN-13: 978-1-4042-3808-4 (lib. bdg.)
  ISBN-10: 1-4042-3808-5 (lib. bdg.)
  1. New Year—Juvenile literature. 2. Holiday decorations—Juvenile literature. 3. Handicraft—Juvenile literature. I. Title.
  GT4905.M46 2008
  394.2614—dc22
                                              2007001029

Manufactured in the United States of America.

Contents

Celebrating a New Year

A new year is a new beginning! On January 1, people around the world **celebrate** the arrival of a new year with fireworks and parties. They look back over the year that ended and think of ways to make the coming year even better.

While most people celebrate the new year of the **Gregorian** calendar on January 1, many people also celebrate new year holidays that fall on other dates. This is because not all calendars start on January 1. For example, the new year in the **traditional** Chinese calendar falls in late January or February.

Can you figure out which new year this girl is celebrating from what she is wearing?

Fun at Midnight

The new year that starts on January 1 begins at midnight, or 12:00 a.m. Therefore, many New Year's celebrations last past midnight. The last day of the old year is New Year's **Eve**. Parents often let their kids stay up until midnight on New Year's Eve. At midnight, people say "Happy New Year" to each other. Many people sing a song called "Auld Lang Syne," which means "times gone by." The song speaks of remembering the past.

People make lots of noise at midnight. Some people hit pots and pans together. Many towns have loud fireworks to welcome the new year.

People gather in New York City's Times Square each New Year's Eve to watch a big ball drop at midnight.

New Year's Day

While there is lots of celebrating at midnight on January 1, there are also traditions that take place later in the day. January 1 is called New Year's Day. People in the southern part of the United States often eat a vegetable called black-eyed peas on New Year's Day. This is said to bring good luck for the rest of the year.

The Tournament of Roses Parade, in Pasadena, California, almost always takes place on New Year's Day. The parade has marching bands and specially trained horses. It also has big **floats** covered with lots of beautiful flowers.

The town of Long Beach, California, made this "A Day at the Beach" float for the Tournament of Roses Parade.

How to Make Snickerdoodles

In the United States, there is a long tradition of serving cookies on New Year's Day. One traditional cookie you can make is the snickerdoodle. Ask an adult to help you use the oven, though.

Turn the oven on to 375° F (190° C). Then mix ½ cup (120 g) butter and ¾ cup (150 g) sugar together in a large bowl like the boy on page 11. Add 1⅓ cups (160 g) flour, 1 teaspoon cream of tartar, ¼ teaspoon salt, and ½ teaspoon baking soda.

Break an egg and add it to the bowl. Keep mixing the dough, or batter, until it forms one big ball.

Mix 2 tablespoons sugar and 1 teaspoon cinnamon in a bowl. Use your hands to roll 1½-inch-(3.8 cm) wide balls of dough. Roll the balls in the cinnamon and sugar.

Put the balls on a cookie sheet. Use a fork to press down the middle of each ball. Bake the cookies for 8 to 10 minutes. Let them cool before serving them, like the cookies on page 11.

New Year's Resolutions

For many people, the new year is a time to make a fresh start. As each new year draws closer, people think about how to make themselves better people. They make New Year's **resolutions** about the things they will do differently in the coming year. Some people promise themselves they will exercise more often. Others decide to learn a new skill or take up an interesting hobby.

Have you ever made a New Year's resolution? Some kids resolve, or promise, to get along better with their brothers or sisters. Other kids decide that they will help their parents more.

Promising to help your parents by washing their car each month is an example of a New Year's resolution.

How to Make a New Year's Scrapbook

New Year's Eve is a great time to look back on the year that is ending. You can make a scrapbook to help you remember the past year.

1 Start by finding an empty notebook. This will be your scrapbook. Write the year that is ending on the cover, or front, of the scrapbook.

2 Ask your parents or neighbors if you can have some old magazines and newspapers to cut up. Cut out pictures of famous people or events from the last year, like the girl on page 15 is doing.

3 Look around your own home for papers to add to your scrapbook. A photo of you and your friends at your birthday party, your school picture, or the ticket from a movie or play you saw would all be good things to use.

4 Take the things that you found or cut out and glue them to the scrapbook's pages. You might want to add drawings of important things that happened to you over the last year, too.

Chinese New Year

While people in China celebrate the new year that starts on January 1, they also celebrate Chinese New Year. The new year celebration lasts 15 days. It begins on the first day of the first month of the traditional Chinese calendar. This calendar is thousands of years old.

Years in the Chinese calendar have numbers and animals tied to them. For example, the Chinese year 4718 is the year of the rat. It begins on January 25, 2020, in the Gregorian calendar. The years of the ox, tiger, rabbit, dragon, snake, horse, sheep, monkey, rooster, dog, and pig follow it.

This dance takes place on the Lantern Festival, which is the fifteenth day of the Chinese New Year celebration.

Celebrating Chinese New Year

Family is an important part of Chinese New Year. It is a time when people visit older family members. People also remember and honor their **ancestors**. Parents give children money in red **envelopes** for Chinese New Year. They hope it will bring good luck since red is a lucky color.

Eating special foods is also part of Chinese New Year. People from southern China eat a sweet cake made from rice. People from northern China eat **dumplings**. Dumplings are supposed to bring good luck because they look like the pieces of gold used for money in China long ago.

These girls are dressed in the lucky color red to take part in a Chinese New Year parade.

Rosh Hashanah

Another important new year is Rosh Hashanah. Rosh Hashanah is the new year in the Jewish calendar. It falls in September or early October. There are many Rosh Hashanah traditions. One such tradition is the blowing of a long horn called a shofar. Shofars are made from the horn of a ram, or male sheep.

Jewish people go to a **synagogue** on Rosh Hashanah. After that, some people go to a body of water, say prayers, and throw bits of bread or other things into the water. Throwing things into the water stands for casting off sins. This practice is called *tashlikh*.

This man is blowing a shofar. People have blown shofars on Rosh Hashanah for thousands of years.

New Year Celebrations Around the World

People in Iran celebrate the new year Norouz on the first day of spring. This falls in late March. People clean their houses, buy flowers, and wear new clothes. They visit each other's houses, eat sweets, and give gifts. In parts of southern India, people celebrate the traditional new year, Puthandu, on April 13 or 14. They eat a big feast and make pictures with rice powder called *kolams*.

People around the world celebrate the new year at different times and in different ways. However, we all look forward to the new beginning a new year brings.

Glossary

ancestors (AN-ses-terz) Family members who lived long ago.

celebrate (SEH-luh-brayt) To honor an important moment by doing special things.

dumplings (DUMP-lingz) Small pieces of dough, or batter, with meat or vegetables inside.

envelopes (EN-veh-lohps) Covers used for mailing letters.

eve (EEV) The evening or day before an important day.

floats (FLOHTS) Low, flat trucks that carry people and sets in a parade.

Gregorian (grih-GOR-ee-un) Having to do with the calendar that starts on January 1 and ends on December 31.

resolutions (reh-zuh-LOO-shunz) Things a person or people decided on and promised to do.

synagogue (SIH-nih-gog) A temple or a house of prayer for Jewish people.

traditional (truh-DIH-shuh-nul) Done in a way that has been passed down over time.

Index

Web Sites

Due to the changing nature of Internet links, PowerKids Press has developed an online list of Web sites related to the subject of this book. This site is updated regularly. Please use this link to access the list:
www.powerkidslinks.com/hfun/nyear/